Women & Legacy
It's More Than You Might Think

Joanne Giardini-Russell

www.thefamilylegacycenter.com

Other books in The Family Legacy Center's series:
Your Living Legacy; An Important Conversation

Copyright © 2014 The Family Legacy Center
All rights reserved.
ISBN-13: 978-1500493189
ISBN-10: 150049318X

Your time is limited, so don't waste it living someone else's life. Don't be trapped by dogma—which is living with the results of other people's thinking. Don't let the noise of others' opinions drown out your own inner voice. And most important, have the courage to follow your heart and intuition. They somehow already know what you truly want to become.

—Steve Jobs, 2005

www.thefamilylegacycenter.com

CONTENTS

	Dedication	vi
1	Women Are from Venus	9
2	Why Legacy Is Important to Women	15
3	Every Family Is Unique	18
4	Divorced Women	22
5	Widowed Women	25
6	Millennials: The Next Generation	28
7	Business Women	32
8	The Need for Legacy-Focused Planning	35
9	My Message to Moms	38
10	Giving Back and Charitable Contributions	42
	Epilogue	45

Women and Legacy: It's More Than You Might Think

DEDICATION

To my children, who inspire my desire to pay attention to my own legacy! Love you all dearly.

To my colleagues and team members —thank you for pushing me to do what I should be doing.

To my parents—I grew up being told that I could accomplish anything that I wanted. It worked. Thank you for the launching pad.

And, to my husband. Thank you for the foundation, freedom and support you consistently provide for my journey. You don't always understand it, but you support me nonetheless! Love you.

Preface

The Legacy Continuum ™

Why this book? At Financial Architects, we focus on retirements for many. We focus on family. We focus on life. We focus on what really matters.

I joined the firm years ago because their process and

www.thefamilylegacycenter.com

their office culture knocked my socks off. Then the fun really began. As time went on, I realized just how many hours in my day were spent learning about the "other" stuff in a family's world. Other stuff meaning family stories, family values, the focus of what the family was and is about —and much more.

That was the fun part! However, as an organization we can't and don't lose sight of how very important building a financial base to fit that family really is. That's what we specialize in.

Along the way, my colleague and friend, Chris Cousins and I founded The Family Legacy Center. Our signature theme is what we refer to as "The Legacy Continuum ™" on the prior page. Note that fifty percent of our work focuses on who a family is, supported by what they have and what they give back. I'll save the greater details for another book! This book shares some of the stories that we heard and what we learned along the way in our journey to bring you The Family Legacy Center. Enjoy.

Joanne Giardini-Russell | Financial Architects, Inc.

joanne@financialarch.com

39395 W. Twelve Mile Rd. Suite 102
Farmington Hills, MI 48331
www.financialarch.com

Is legacy important to you? www.thefamilylegacycenter.com

1
Women Are from Venus

In 1992, Dr. John Gray released the best-selling book *Men Are from Mars, Women Are from Venus*. In it, Gray provides tips and tools men and women can use to communicate with each other better. In his view, the starting point for improving communication between men and women was to acknowledge the differences between their needs, desires and behaviors.

Fast forward to 2014. Not much has changed! We can still apply an awareness of how gender influences communication—and Dr. Gray's tips and tools—to just about every area of life. Women and men see many things differently. Is that a bad thing? Not necessarily.

My financial-planning colleague, Chris Cousins, and I founded The Family Legacy Center in 2013. We were driven to create it because we found ourselves returning again and again to the same pivotal question: "At the end of the rainbow, isn't there more than just a pot of dollars?" Our combined thirty-five years of experience in the finance and insurance arena and a zillion client hours told us that the answer was a resounding *yes*. But how could we put our certainty into action?

The Family Legacy Center was born out of our shared desire to help individuals, families, and businesses better facilitate legacy discussions. That's a vital process because once you clarify your legacy goals, it becomes easier to focus your daily choices and design your financial world around what you ultimately want that legacy to mean to your family and friends. Legacy is a far-reaching notion and you have the opportunity to define and shape yours into exactly what you want it to be.

Chris and I believed women had a significantly different perspective on legacy than men. So our initial interviews and research started with that premise. When we launched our new endeavor, we spent our first six months interviewing only women. (Chris, being male, definitely agreed that women are different than men!) We asked women to describe their thoughts about leaving a legacy and how they believe men and women differ in their views on the topic.

Let's take a moment to define this term, *legacy*. Most people conjure up the image of a recently passed ninety-three-year-old man, a stack of legal documents obtained from his safe, and a family waiting in a sterile room for the reading of the will. That's not the version of legacy that I'm addressing.

At The Family Legacy Center we define legacy as *living*. Legacy is what you're living today. Legacy is also what you're building with your life and how you're doing it. Ultimately your legacy does incorporate what you leave behind in this world—which can be money and possessions, but more importantly, values, experiences, ideas, businesses built, and so on. We can't ignore the fact that we leave parts of our lives behind—good and bad. The key is that you get to decide which it will be.

When I ask men about legacy, they're often focused on assets that are passed to a next generation. Those assets can be in the form of cash, a business, etc. For men, legacy frequently equates to physical things that can be seen and quantified.

When I ask women about legacy, their minds will often turn to family-focused goals or activities. How did her children turn out? Did she do a good job of passing values and experiences to them? Are they good, responsible adults? Will her grandchildren remember her?

Women and Legacy: It's More Than You Might Think

Then, when I ask a twenty-something? Legacy to them is so far down the road that they usually just give me a puzzled look! Their stage of life has them focusing on building careers and families.

Even though every person on the planet—whether they're one or one hundred—will leave a legacy. Most people just don't slow down enough to realize that they have the ability to design their own legacy, whatever shape it may take.

One of my clients, Molly Green, puts it this way:

Actually, the topic of the eulogy given by me at my husband's funeral was "Legacy." For me it means a few things. It means passing good lessons and values to my children. I want to be able to say that I did something else besides myself. I want to constantly educate myself. I want to show them some kind of volunteering or charitable activity and be known for helping others. My goal is for my kids to turn out OK.

Molly's husband had committed suicide three years earlier. She was raising four young children, returning to the workforce, and she and her family were among the subjects of a documentary film called *Transforming Loss*. Molly found that helping others grieve helped her and her children to grieve as well. Molly, intentionally or not, has taken huge steps in building her own legacy.

Another client, Sharman, lost her husband Phil to interstitial lung disease. Sharman says:

I view legacy as something left behind, but it's made up of little pieces of all the people that have touched our lives. To this day (eight years later) I still hear and meet people that Phil touched. I think if a person is able to leave that type of connection behind, it's huge. It doesn't have to be a building. And, my view of legacy changes over time. I'm exploring my life and becoming someone different than I was when I was married to Phil. So, I'll be touching others in a different manner.

Since Phil passed, Sharman has founded and operates The FACES (Family and Caregiver Education and Support) Foundation in his memory. She often presents the PHIL (Pulmonary Health and Illness of the Lung) Award, which honors outstanding respiratory therapists at various hospitals. Further information about Sharman's foundation and the PHIL Award can be found at thefacesfoundation.org.

Molly and Sharman exemplify the mindset that we've discovered many women share. They plan for the future, they plan for their children and families, and they plan for their own extra-family activities. They control their legacies by which activities they choose. Each woman chooses different paths based on her personal history and personality.

In our planning and work with clients, we often talk about ripple effects—the consequences, short-term and long-term, of either doing or not doing something. Though they may start out as insignificant blips, some of those ripples grow into powerful waves that can have a big impact. Molly and Sharman are excellent examples of how the ripple effect can lead to powerful legacies.

Think of a time when you may have taken a friend to lunch to hear about a problem she was having with her child. The advice you offered, in her mind, was fabulous and she went home to her family with a new perspective. You may have changed the course of the relationship between your friend and her child. Maybe the lesson or challenge was so significant that the child will remember it thirty years later when she becomes a parent herself. Your lunchtime chat may have more lasting effects than you realize. Daily actions like that are one way you build your legacy.

Women and Legacy: It's More Than You Might Think

Planning for the ripple effect is a central idea we coach our clients through at The Family Legacy Center. We use tools that identify what kind of ripples you want to create and help you discover ways to amplify that ripple outward into the world.

Watching the dynamics between men and women during our meetings is fascinating. And as a planning team, Chris and I often see different sides of the same coin. Our process takes the best of the best from both husband and wife and helps them lay the foundation for their shared legacy. We help pinpoint, capture, and express their unique perspective on legacy. It's an extremely rewarding process for all involved.

I think of this book as part of my legacy. I hope women will read it and identify even one idea that stirs a desire to think, create, plan, and enhance their own legacy planning. In the coming chapters, I discuss the roles of women in many capacities, and I believe every female reader will be able to relate to one or more of the situations I describe.

My overarching intention is to spark thought and encourage discussion about individual and family legacy—an effort that's lacking in our fast-paced, distracted world. Working within the financial-planning arena has led me to drastically change how I plan and think of legacy. I'm all too aware of the downsides of failing to plan.

Today, I'm confident that if I left the planet tomorrow, my family would have all the resources they need to continue a happy life. Would they miss me? Of course they would. But would they be prepared with values, experiences, work ethics and financial resources? Absolutely.

Knowing that I've protected my family from most of the risks they could encounter is a very confident and rewarding place to be in. That's the essence of why I'm committed to my work and why I've dedicated myself to building The Family

Legacy Center.

CHALLENGE QUESTION:

Ask your spouse to define his/her version of legacy. Keep the door open for any discussion that could follow.

2

Why Legacy Is Important to Women

Let's first acknowledge that legacy is important to everyone—men and women alike. My focus here, though, is a discussion of women and legacy.

During The Family Legacy Center's initial research, we explored these central questions: What does the word *legacy* mean to you? How do you make your legacy become what you want it to be? And how might you see legacy differently than men might? The vast majority of the women we interviewed were interested in legacy as it related to two primary areas: 1) the footprint they will leave as an individual, and 2) their children and grandchildren.

Many women discussed a desire to have a positive impact on someone or something during their lifetime. When we stop to consider, we understand that every person will have an impact on someone else during the course of a lifetime.

Consider, for example, your grandmother. I'd be willing to bet a lot of money that she had an impact on someone you know, possibly you. She may have had a great impact or a minor one on you, but almost certainly she had a major impact on someone somewhere. Could that impact have been a negative one? Perhaps. If so, are there ways a negative impact might have been altered? Of course. Your grandmother could have learned a different behavior that might have changed her actions.

My point isn't to villainize hypothetical grandmothers, but to point out that we can control how we impact the people in our lives. A woman is never too young to start acknowledging that she will leave a legacy that will influence someone over a lifetime. Don't discount the little things.

Allie Smith of The Latchkey Mom blog (thelatchkeymom.com) has a wonderful way with words. She is the mother of four children, one of whom is autistic. She writes about the reality of being a mother. She writes from the heart. Allie has been published in various new publications and recently garnered a $5,000 donation to her child's school following an article she wrote about autism. Allie displays a passion for many things in her world, but she says her main passion is her children. Her footprint on the world is transparently tied to her children. She continues to do great things and her impact will be enormous.

Our conversations with women often circled back to the topic of children or grandchildren. Mothers are generally and stereotypically the family caretakers and nurturers. It came as no surprise that their efforts on that front were often discussed as an important element of their legacy. We heard many variations of: "I want my children to become good people"; "I want to provide a little financial help to my children if I can"; and "I want my children to remember me fondly."

One client expressed her desire to fund her grandchildren's education. We put into place a permanent life insurance policy and changed the language in her trust that provided these funds for her grandchildren's education. Done. Problem solved. We suggested that she determine a new legacy goal since that one was solved. Legacy accomplishments can be as simple as a stroke of pen on paper, or they may be as subtle as a lifelong series of conversations over the kitchen table. Just about everything we choose to do contributes to our legacy.

Taking a proactive approach to strategizing what you want your legacy to be can make it that much easier to ensure it will be what you want. The keys are to identify your goals and begin a lifetime action plan. One client had a succinct way to sum it up: "You may very well have to plan financially today to achieve your legacy goals later in life."

Teaching is an essential component of our legacy discussions. Sometimes we're teaching the client. Sometimes our clients are teaching us. Most women want to know their children are financially secure and successful, which requires learning on the child's part and teaching on the parents' part. We often work with the second generation of a family in our planning practice. In those instances, the parents and the advisor team hope to launch young adults into the world from the most solid platform available to them.

I want to emphasize that most women we talked to placed leaving money to their children—whether the amount in question was significant or modest—only as a bonus. It wasn't something they were enormously focused on. One woman said, "I wouldn't want to leave my kids a ton of money because they'd get lazy. I'd like to leave them a little something, but I'd rather they understand things. I'd rather they have good habits and good financial understanding so they can create their own pile of money."

Remember, at the end of the life rainbow, there's more than a pot of gold. Most women hope there's a pot of gold *and* evidence of the kind of life they wanted to live. The pot of gold just isn't the main goal for most women.

And, who's to say that pot at the end of the rainbow will even go to her children! Many women expressed a desire to give charitably, a topic I explore more fully in a separate chapter.

CHALLENGE QUESTION:

If you could only pass along two of the following to your children, which would you leave out and why: a) values that you have taught, b) experiences you have given, and c) money.

3

Every Family Is Unique

Boy, is that an understatement. Families are like snowflakes. No two are alike.

The Family Legacy Center works with individuals, couples, retirees, businesses, and the entire family structure. We are engaged in a broad and fascinating range of conversations. That's what makes my job so enjoyable, actually. Because we're involved in such a broad spectrum of conversations, we've developed tools that can help everyone involved. Communication styles are enhanced, goals are defined, and action plans are created. What's better than having everybody "on board" with their family plan?

We have some great family stories within our client base. One of those is the Thompson family of northern Michigan. Jeff Thompson was nineteen years old when his hobby of crafting skis became a full-time endeavor. It was never the family's intention to build a family business around Jeff's love of making skis but his mom, Shari, says, "I've never worked so many hours for so little pay and had so much fun doing it."

The Thompson family has enormous legacy goals, whether or not they have fully articulated them. They are building their empire, as big or small as they'd like it to be, for themselves and for their generations of their family. They leverage each individual's strengths and put them to their best use. Visit their website (sccskis.com) to learn more. They're a very fun family!

We frequently work with blended families who have their own unique challenges. I have a blended family. Three children are mine (ages twenty, eighteen, and fifteen as I write this) and two are my husband's (ages sixteen and twelve). Living as a blended family can take a great deal of patience for all involved. It requires a long list of skills—zipping your lips when necessary, respecting different parenting styles, sharing bedrooms, and much more! Success as a blended family is complicated. Everyone arrives to a newly blended household with different backgrounds, experiences, and ideas. My children moved into a house they didn't grow up in, which wasn't easy for them. My husband and his kids instantly had three extra children in their home, which wasn't easy for them.

I'll never forget the arguments we had over shoes when we first moved in. Yes, shoes. We married, moved in together, and suddenly there were more than the two pairs of shoes (his prior setup) sitting next to the back door. He couldn't understand it. The math seemed obvious to me: seven bodies multiplied by a pair of shoes each equals fourteen shoes on the floor. So what? But it took months for us to reach a good shoe equilibrium!

So if shoes can be a trying issue, imagine how challenging financial planning could be. Not to mention setting long-term goals, creating fairness, and negotiating established parenting styles. Imagine the stress that can emerge out of a blended family situation! Can we fix all the potential trouble spots of financial planning for blended families? Not always—but we can help make sure each gets a measure of attention.

I believe estate planning for blended families requires special attention and sensitivity. I encourage you to find a very skilled estate-planning attorney who has experience in this area. I've heard countless stories about bad estate (i.e., legacy) planning in these instances. Don't let that be your family. At The Family Legacy Center, we make enormous efforts to work with highly trained and experienced estate-planning attorneys who can draft, in accordance with the law, documents that reflect your wishes.

The Family Legacy Center also works with families without children. Being part of a couple with no children or being a person who is childless has no less meaning in the legacy department. For example, people without children may have more dollars to deliver toward a charitable legacy—which is one way the ripple effects of their financial legacies may be felt for years to come.

According to CNN.com, in 2012 the average cost of raising a child in the U.S. reached a whopping $240,080. With our five children, that totals more than $1,200,000 that we might have available to leave to a charity, a hospital, build a building, or have perpetual scholarships established at our alma maters, Michigan State University and the University of Michigan.

Is that what we would choose to do? I have no idea. But it's an option we don't have right now. We pay for college. Part of our family legacy is paying for college for each of our kids. Every choice is a trade-off. The best part of this choice is that we get to see where the resources go and how they influence the children. That's an important part of what legacy planning means to me.

No matter what your family's particular features and challenges, the entire landscape—every person, every role, every business, every financial account—must be paid attention to for the family or business to achieve their ultimate legacy plan. Going forward, everything a family does as a unit should adhere to the legacy plan you've crafted.

Once a legacy plan is in place, it's easier to make decisions. For example, should a business be created? Perhaps, if it fits into your long-term legacy goals. Should a child study overseas? Perhaps, if it fits the long-term educational goals of the family. Should a scholarship fund be created? Perhaps, if it fits the long-term family philanthropic goals. It's easier to evaluate a plan or opportunity when you have something to measure it against!

The absolute best part of family legacy planning is all that it can create for a family unit. It's amazing what a group engaged in a common mission can accomplish. Imagine the security that a family member can feel knowing that her choices are supported by the parameters of the family's mutual goals. Which is not to say that a family legacy can't have its share of challenges and complications if one of its members doesn't buy in. But that's a topic for a different e-book!

CHALLENGE QUESTION:

Are you working toward accomplishing a set of family goals? Have you ever created a list of family goals and then written a family living legacy statement?

4

Divorced Women

Divorced women may find themselves in a difficult financial position following a divorce. Divorce doesn't always have a negative financial impact on a woman, but in the majority of divorces I've encountered in my work, the woman is the party who typically suffers financially.

Attorney Denise Couling, of Couling Law & Mediation, PLLC, discusses her observations on divorced women in general. Couling finds that women often shortchange their own financial futures in the process of serving the needs of their husbands and children while married. This limits their futures, personally as well as financially, in ways women often don't anticipate.

This is especially evident when a marriage becomes troubled. Couling explains, "Few things can be more rewarding than being part of a family that works together to love and support their children while also honoring each parties' career or interests." While everyone would prefer for all marriages to be happy ones that stand the test of time, that simply isn't always the reality.

Couling observes, "Even a husband and wife who have divorced can continue on as partners in a successful 'joint venture' in supporting their children's futures while pursuing independent paths in life. When a marriage can't be saved, the question often is, are both parties in a position to go forward with their lives on positive financial—and personal—footing?" For many women, sadly, too often the answer is no, or not without some dramatic changes."

Couling goes on to note, "What I would say to every woman, whether married, a mother or not, is to *never* lose sight of the value of having your own career and interests. It

Women and Legacy: It's More Than You Might Think

is so sad to see a woman who once was confident and earned an excellent income remain in an oppressive or unhappy relationship because she dropped out of the workforce and she no longer feels that she is attractive to employers or able to support herself."

In Couling's observation, *everyone*, regardless of gender or marital status, is a better "advocate for themselves" and can navigate their future with more optimism and options when she (or he) maintains a lifeline to a career, volunteer activities, skills, and even hobbies that readily translate into employability. "Sometimes the pressures of family life make the stay-at-home option the best one for a period of time—especially when children are very young. Just don't lose sight of how good it feels to be the pilot of your own future."

Why am I focusing on financial stability and planning in connection with divorced women? Because it can be difficult to get back on your feet following a divorce. It can take a period of time to get financially acclimated to the new way of life. Going through a divorce and the financial upset that it may cause can produce something of a "two steps forward and one step back" feeling for a woman's legacy plan.

I enjoy working with divorced women as clients, perhaps because I was one. I understand their challenges. I understand what they're trying to accomplish and where they're attempting to go.

A divorced parent's job isn't easy. I'll never forget the moment my daughter learned that my financial situation wasn't always ideal. I divorced when she was eight years old. As a sixteen-year-old, we were sitting with my parents having a pretty adult conversation when she said, "I didn't realize at the time that it was difficult for you." I understood in that moment that I'd accomplished my goal. My kids didn't see life any differently than when their dad was in the house. I want them to absorb a "carry on despite adversity" attitude. It worked.

Deep down I know that my children got a different view of their mother having gone through those years together. We made lemonade out of our crop of lemons. Without needing to discuss the difficulties, my choices and actions—and theirs—during that time conveyed values, strength, and focus to my children. These are skills they will always be able draw on.

Does the fact that a person is divorced preclude them from having family legacy desires? Of course not. In fact, I might argue that going through a rough time can make women stronger, more resilient, and even more determined to plan and implement her legacy. But, it certainly may take some catch-up time for a woman who has gone through a divorce to get back on her feet and then have the time, energy and resources to focus on her legacy.

CHALLENGE QUESTION:

This one is more challenge than question. During the time surrounding a divorce, do what you can to be close to your children. I enjoyed the time period when it was just me and my three children—we had fun dinners and watched TV and just did whatever we wanted to do together. I was the sole leader of the family and we became extremely close, a unit of togetherness. Embrace your divorce, if you can. Find the best parts and relish them. You may not be able to imagine right now how this could be true, but life will change and you'll fondly remember those times.

5

Widowed Women

Many people assume that a widow and a divorced woman share similar attitudes toward life and legacy concerns. I haven't found that to be true among my clients. Women in both situations have experienced loss but most of the time (and I acknowledge I'm generalizing here), the immediate and long-term pressures are more intense for women who are widowed.

Widows, in my opinion, experience a longer period of mending and healing than divorced women usually require. Is that to be expected? It all depends. Was her spouse ill for years? Was her spouse killed in a car accident or another unexpected event? Were the couple's documents left in order or was she left with a legal mess to manage on top of grieving and perhaps caring for children who are also grieving. An individual widow's challenges and responsibilities can take on so many different features that we should avoid assumptions.

Often, when a spouse has passed away, I'll learn the widow wasn't included in any established estate-planning process. Sometimes she didn't pay any of the bills. She may not know the passwords for their joint accounts. She may not know where to find account statements and other files. I recall one friend who was left with a safe deposit box key. To where? She had no idea. It remains a mystery to this day.

For months and months, in addition to a new way to navigate her personal life, many widows are also discovering new life skills. She is still grieving while also balancing the stresses of learning important new things. What if she has a full-time job that she still must tend to? More pressure. What if she has young children? Even more pressure. With all of these extra pressures, we can only hope the family finances were left in very good shape—or else.

Are you a recent widow? Don't worry about your legacy right now! I understand that you probably don't care about that right now and that you have a full plate. I know that you'll surprise me—and almost certainly yourself—by being tougher than you think. After whatever period of time is right for you, you'll gain clarity in your new world and move forward on your journey toward your own legacy. It's a difficult and long process, but you'll get there.

As part of our research, we spoke to Micki. Micki's husband Fred had been ill for a period of time and finally passed away. She told us that she was initially concerned about whether or not she'd be able to support herself. She wondered, "Will I be able to keep my house and keep my life the way it is today?" But Micki went on to share:

> Fred always tried to prepare me for the day that he wouldn't be here. He worked hard to 'cross-train' me, if you will. I really didn't want to learn any of it. But, at Fred's insistence, I did shadow him often and learn what I could—whether it was fixing something small or learning something new about our finances, I did it. To this day, I wake and say, *Thank you, Fred.* He prepared me for my new life, he left me a legacy.

Fred's trust and documents were in good order. Micki was fortunate to have a relatively easy time with the legal and financial items she had to handle. Fred had children from a prior marriage so while he was still alive, he and Micki made changes to his trust. Micki encouraged Fred to keep things "fair," to use her word, so that her ongoing relationships with her stepchildren would be positive. They are. The last time we talked to Micki, she'd just had a phone call that her stepdaughter was expecting a new baby. Micki tells everyone how fortunate she was that Fred thought things through carefully and planned for her future.

Women and Legacy: It's More Than You Might Think

So how does legacy relate to widows? Many women turn into amazing creatures after losing a spouse. I believe they even surprise themselves at times. The immense respect that they often gain from their children, friends, and family helps shore up her new world. Eventually she finds her way to her next chapter.

Widows have the ability to choose, create, and navigate toward their own legacies unencumbered and unchallenged. Meaning that they were once part of a twosome, but are now solo. Many discover it can be a little easier to focus on their legacy goals, since those goals emerge out of one person's vision and require less compromise.

Remember Sharman, the woman who lost her husband Phil? She went on to create the successful FACES Foundation in his honor that she runs with a passion. There is an annual golf fundraiser and dozens of other events each year to support the PHIL Award. Her foundation has hired a staff. Sharman created jobs, awareness, recognition for caregivers who often go largely unnoticed and more. But, the most important thing she has done was for herself and for Phil—keeping his memory alive. Did Sharman ever dream that she would end up running a foundation one day? No. But she created her next chapter and has done a spectacular job of playing it out.

CHALLENGE QUESTION:

If you are a recently widowed female, go easy on yourself! I hope your situation didn't leave you in a financial bind or with a legal mess. I hope you have the time and resources to pick up the pieces and go on. I hope you help other widows navigate an area that worked out well for you or that was a particular challenge—for example, finances. Reach out to other women and offer your advice. They can use it!

6

Millenials: The Next Generation

These gals are fun! I adore the millennials. The world is their oyster and they're ready to take it on.

I wish I could have known at their age what I know now. I know, I know—that's how life works. But, moms, please start talking to these gals earlier about planning, goals, and the like. When they identify their goals and create a roadmap that aligns with their values, experiences, and their financial outlook—they'll go places we couldn't have dreamed for them.

A newer client recently told me, "I never thought we'd achieve what we did. It's rewarding, it's amazing and I'm blessed." What a wonderful thing to be able to say. Arriving at wealth may allow you to take that next step to "achieve beyond expectations." At that stage you may have the ability to focus on charitable contributions, foundations, personal endeavors and so much more. But planning in the early years is what allows you to "arrive" at wealth. It's vital that we get the younger generations focused on planning as early as possible.

Take Erica. She's building her empire with her project-based personal assistant company, Gal Friday, LLC (therealgalfriday.com). I asked her to write a little about what the concept of legacy means to her:

> Legacies are for rock stars and rich people. People who own airlines and islands and buy football teams because they're bored. People who go to Yale or Princeton and buy Christian Louboutins like they're toilet paper. At least that's what I used to think. Before I was a business owner, before I had to think about my son going to college. Before I realized I

had my own legacy, just by living.

I am 35, and I wish someone would have told me about legacy ten years ago. I always had a preconceived notion that I would worry about and plan for the future later. (I was too busy living my life.) Well *now* is later and, unknowingly, I have been building my legacy this whole time. Lucky for me, I'm surrounded by people who help me be a better person, and in turn, live for a better legacy.

I grew up in a standard household in the 1980s. Blue-collar income, three siblings, a dog, two fish, a hamster. My mom was a stay-at-home hero and my father's family had owned an insurance company since 1935. I always thought I would grow up and go into the family business (it was part of my preplanned legacy), but then life happened. Unexpectedly, life happened. We all ended up going our separate ways, my dad lost the business, and I was left to find a new way. A new legacy.

Legacy is a funny thing. It happens whether you want it to or not. When I was nineteen, I was working in a high-end restaurant, preparing to be a chef because of my love for food (part of my legacy). When I was in my twenties, I became a mother and it taught me how to care for other people (part of my legacy). In 2001, I jump-started my career and refused to take no for answer (part of my legacy). In 2010, I was married outside, in a park, in downtown Detroit because I love to be unconventional (part of my legacy). Three years ago, I started my own business because someone told me I couldn't (my favorite part of my legacy).

I have learned that legacy happens whether we want it to or not. It is *who we are* and *how we live*. We are leaving stories, memories, traditions, and a life, but we are leaving it to those who will still be living. My son, his children, their children, and even their children will know who I was and why I lived, because of my legacy. I choose to build that legacy myself, instead of letting it get built without me.

Erica is an example of these younger gals who have powerful new tools—mainly technology—at their disposal. Life can be easier in some respects, yet more difficult in others. Though technology can help in so many ways, it can become a diffuser in many cases as well. How many dinners have you shared with your twelve-year-old who is hiding a phone under the table so she can Instagram her friends?

In a short aside, I want to confess that I adore technology, but I think it's often important to step back, pull out paper and pen, and have a good conversation with family, friends, and clients. There's power in an old-fashioned yellow legal pad and your ears—and when we return to those simpler methods we can yield amazing results! At The Family Legacy Center, we take a lot of time to listen to our clients. If we aren't listening, we're unable to help them craft a path to their goals. Listening carefully is a pretty simple notion. But is it done well very often? Not really.

So how do these millennial gals navigate the typical demands of parenthood, jobs, and technology while keeping a legacy in the back of their minds? We'll often sit with a woman in this age group to devise a five-year vision statement. What do they see their world looking like in five years? The exercise gives them a vision to work toward. Then we step back and determine what needs to be done today to realize their vision. We look to values, experiences, goals, jobs, financials—everything is fair game and, ideally, every aspect contributes to the journey toward the five-year vision.

It might sound like a simple process, but it can be an arduous task that requires difficult questions and equally difficult answers. We need to ask the right question at the proper time and then help align clients' resources with their individual visions. At this point in their world, it's really important to help them understand the value in long-term planning. We need to emphasize the importance of protecting their young families. If this group of young women is smart enough to plan ahead and plan well, the world is theirs to conquer!

CHALLENGE QUESTION:

Have you developed your personal network of professional advisors to help you plan how you can achieve your goals? These are the best years to assemble a phenomenal team dedicated to helping you realize your vision.

7

Business Women

Men often identify the building of a business as a great part of their legacy. Well, not to be outdone, many women feel the same way.

Meet Ashley Watterson, founder of Tocca Massage Therapy (toccamassage.com). Ashley was in her early twenties when she dreamed of and created her business:

> I had purchased a home by my early twenties and was starting my business when, in 2008, the economy crashed. Because it crashed around me, I found myself becoming more conservative. I don't live beyond my means. I do things that I value such as travel and running marathons, but in the back of my mind, I'm always saving for that rainy day or the day I can retire early because of all that I've created.

> When I first opened Tocca, I had my mind set to have a number of locations and create a large organization. With time, I'm finding my values are changing to some degree. Other things are having more importance in my world. I realize that I can't always control business events like I can control my marathon training schedule. I have a significant other in my world today and more. Life is becoming more about other important things versus creating a giant business. What I value most in my business is the relationships that have been created. When a client says that they couldn't live without Tocca? Well, that's what I want Tocca to be.

Tocca will grow along with Ashley and her world. Women often have a healthy life-balance approach to work and business. Blending the two is an art and one that many women value. I don't think enough credit is given to working mothers—even after twenty years of society telling us we should appreciate and applaud them. Work and motherhood require a constant and virtuosic balancing act.

Attorney Adrienne Knack of Williams & Associates, P.C., is a powerhouse. Adrienne and her husband have a two-year-old daughter named Lily. Adrienne is also the "legacy" of Tim Williams. Tim is the founder of Williams & Associates and eventually Adrienne will be filling his shoes, as he likes to say.

Adrienne intends to grow the practice—now and in the future. She'll work to expand her client base and, according to her, "create a life." A great part of what she is creating has been designed to do what she loves (practice law) *and* show her daughter that:

Yes, you can have both a strong career and a happy, well-adjusted family. Will Lily be the one who fills my shoes one day? That would be great, but, if not, I'll have a succession plan in place.

There is working-mom guilt at times. But Lily is cared for by her father, her grandparents, and her babysitter. I'll never forget a law-school class—Family Law—in which the professor said that it is not necessarily healthy to have a child raised only by immediate family members. That stuck with me and I'd have to agree. We like to mix it up for our daughter's care so she experiences different people and different things.

For Adrienne, it all about prioritizing and balancing. Her work, her practice, her entire career is and will become increasingly part of her vast legacy. She is valued, respected, and extremely important to her clients, her employees, and her family.

What I enjoy most about both Ashley and Adrienne is that they're actively planning their lives and impending legacies. It is something they consciously consider and articulate, and their quests to reach their legacy goals are counterbalanced by their values, family situations, and lifestyle choices.

CHALLENGE QUESTION:

Are you doing what you want to be doing? If you're a working mother, ensure that your career is brought into balance by your values, goals, and intentions.

Sometimes we working women get so caught up in the daily chaos that we don't take moments to pull back to watch our lives unfold. Make a quarterly date with yourself to reflect on your life and growing legacy and make changes where appropriate.

8

The Need for Legacy-Focused Planning

I was on a conference call recently in which a gentleman said, "If you want something that you've never had before, you have to do something that you've never done before." Those are the words of Lou Cassara of The Cassara Clinic, an Illinois-based professional development organization.

The statement is simple, but enormous. In today's world, we've all been conditioned to want things instantaneously with relatively little work. But not much has changed over the last few hundred years: If you want something, you'll have to work toward it. Remember the classic definition of insanity—doing the same thing over and over and expecting a different result? Well, as Cassara points out, if we want something different for ourselves, we should do things differently.

How does that relate to legacy? If you want to create a positive legacy (rather than a negative legacy that is simply "left behind"), how you navigate your life can have an enormous impact. The Family Legacy Center wants you to *live* your legacy. Why bother building one if you aren't enjoying the ride?

That's the foundational idea of The Family Legacy Center. We are willing and able to help our clients make solid financial decisions that will help them build their fortunes— but we're dedicated to engaging in conversations about *why* we're all working so hard to fill that pot of gold at the end of rainbow.

Our conversations within The Family Legacy Center are a natural extension of financial planning, in my opinion. When we align family values, desires, experiences, and charitable desires with financial resources, the whole process comes to light. In fact, I'd even say it comes to *life*. At our reviews it's extremely rewarding to hear "we achieved this goal because we followed our family's legacy vision statement." The pot of gold at the end of the rainbow is filled with more than dollars. Our planning process reflects our certainty that it also holds our values, charitable activities, and more.

What exactly is a family's legacy vision statement? After in-depth discovery, we are able to craft a document that the family can operate by. Much like a company mission statement, the family legacy vision statement exists to direct the family's actions and keep them on track. Life can be simpler for everyone if we know where we are trying to go. Decisions are easier to make and goals are more easily attained. Maybe these documents are reviewed annually at a family retreat, or during a vacation, or in a conference room. We'll help facilitate whatever works best for the family.

Part of what I consider legacy-focused planning is the incorporation of what is commonly referred to as an ethical will. What is that and why should you create one? I'll tell you about mine. When I describe mine to my clients there's almost always a thoughtful "ahh" of understanding. I created a document that has my message, if you will, to my family if anything should happened to me suddenly. Everybody knows where the document is, but they haven't read it. It begins, "If you're reading this...." I inject what I think is humor. To my daughter, for example, I write, "Don't buy any more clothes with the insurance proceeds—you have enough." But my joking tone is designed to inject values as well as levity.

In my ethical will I write about not wanting a funeral. I just don't like them. The intent of these pages, which I revise a few times a year, is to guide my family and make managing the loss much easier for them. How many times has an accident occurred and you saw the family go through a horrible time wondering about the deceased's wishes. A trust is full of legal instructions (which are extremely important, of course), but the ethical will can serve as a sort of "cover page" to the trust documents. A trustee for the trust will likely appreciate the document as it may make his or her job easier.

What do you include in an ethical will? Anything goes. Common elements are a story you want passed along, values you want to restate, instructions to children (be nice to others, etc). It's your document and anything goes. I find that writing and rewriting this document gives me a sense of peace. I'm able to add and delete things without restating my legal trust. The ethical will is a helpful bridge to the trust documents.

Another example of a great thing to include in an ethical will is an explanation of why funds have been left to a philanthropic cause instead of family members. Remember, this document is your chance to explain yourself. Take the opportunity to do so because it will serve your family well. Trust me, I've seen bad outcomes when there are no explanations.

On The Family Legacy Center's website, which you can find at thefamilylegacycenter.com, there's a link to the Ethical Will Builder document. I encourage you to go online to check it out and then begin building your ethical will today. Or email me directly at joanne@financialarch.com and I'll send it to you.

CHALLENGE QUESTION:

Have you thought about your family's wealth and estate planning aside from an annual review with your financial professional? If not, think about why you haven't done so. If so, congratulations. Please help someone close to you by suggesting they do the same.

9

My Message to Moms

Because this is my book, I'm going to unapologetically sneak in another message. The name of this chapter is not meant to exclude women who aren't mothers by any means, but much of the message involves our roles as mothers.

Roles. Only one of our roles is being a parent. I recall when I was starting college in 1983, the "women can have it all" campaign was everywhere in the United States. I thought I was in the heart of the campaign and felt as if its message was entirely directed to me alone!

I had seen the film *Baby Boom* in which Diane Keaton has a baby land in her world, but she still works and juggles everything (apparently). I was brainwashed. Remember, I was a young college girl and life was carefree.

I wanted to be a pilot, an attorney (because I read a good novel with a female attorney as the lead and I wanted her life), or a doctor. So, I went to school at Michigan State University and picked marketing as my major. Not even close to a pilot, attorney, or doctor.

I graduated and accidentally landed in the marketing department of an insurance company. I, like the rest of the world, didn't like insurance. I thought it was a boring product that people pretty much universally dislike. When you're dealing with clients over a product they dislike, there's not a lot of warm and fuzzy going around!

I wasn't quite sure where I was going, but quickly felt that the world was really saying "you *can't* have it all" not "you *can* have it all." I met my future husband, we married, and we started a family. I had my first child at 28 and was sure at that point that having it all was a delusion in our society. Something has to give. You're going to give up something someplace. There are just twenty-four hours in a day. You either spend less time with your spouse, your children, or your job. And that's OK. There's too much pressure to try and have it all. I say, have what you want instead of trying to have it all. And be your best at the parts that you choose.

I spent the next eight years running my own small business, one that my three children could grow up in—a children's resale shop. They loved it; they hated it. They worked in it as teenagers—after it was sold to a family friend. The business still exists, it's in its twenty-second year. That's more than can be said of many companies!

After selling the store, I became a divorced mom of three kids, ages ten, eight, and five. I hadn't planned for that circumstance, but there it was.

I spent the next six years getting on my feet in many ways. Parenting-wise. Financially. Emotionally. I dated a man with two children of his own and finally we married. We now have five children ranging in age from twelve to twenty-one. During the time I was divorced and single, my children and I became what I'd consider extra close. I can actually look back and say we had a good time in those years.

I merged into the insurance and financial industry, an industry I knew from previous experience, but disliked. How did that happen?

Well, long story short: I've grown to be a huge advocate of planning. Of everything related to planning. Simple insurance planning. Simple financial planning. Simple estate planning. Then moving up to the complex rungs of each area. It's so very important. As you age, you start to see a broader view of how life plays out. So here's my simple message: *plan.*

Plan for your own world, even if your spouse isn't on the same page. Do what you can. Does he have life insurance that would allow you and your children to be OK if something happened? I know, he doesn't like to talk about it. He thinks that you'll just become "rich" and share it with your next husband. I know, he thinks that $150,000 of group life insurance offered through his job will last you and the three kids forever. (Good luck with that.) I've heard it all!

What if he developed severe arthritis and couldn't work for three years? Are you prepared to live on $3,500 a month instead of the $10,000 you're accustomed to? Would it still be possible to keep the kids in their sports and other activities? Probably not. Ask the tough questions—and *plan*.

Be involved during your annual meetings with your financial professional. Know your advisor. Know the basics even if you don't like numbers. Go to the meeting and daydream through the entire session if need be, but at least get yourself comfortable with possibility of contacting that person if something goes wrong.

Establish a phenomenal team of players to work with you and your family through life. Have a great estate-planning attorney, a great financial person, a great CPA, a great banker, a great insurance agent and others. Make sure these people know their craft and are confident enough in their abilities to work as a team. If one of them throws another team member under the bus? Fire him or her. You're the leader of your team, they're not. They can be replaced rather easily.

Guide your children. Talk to them about the big things when you feel they've reached an appropriate age. Talk about dollars, plans, jobs, economics, and setting goals. Even if your kids don't want to learn, as the parent, you should learn enough to be able to coach them along the way. My kids have plans in place that I didn't even know about until I was forty. Do you think my kids will have a better long-term economic life than I did? You betcha. And guess what, that's part of my legacy.

CHALLENGE QUESTION:

No question. Just take this chapter to heart! Go find a good financial advisor and do some estate planning. Now. No excuses.

And write that ethical will. You will love (or at least grow to love) having it in place.

10

Giving Back and Charitable Contributions

This final chapter addresses charitable endeavors. I'm ending with this topic because a part of me feels that co-founding The Family Legacy Center fulfills a part of my charitable desires. It is certainly not a charity. Full disclosure: The Family Legacy Center is a for-profit LLC.

However, the discussions we foster and what we bring families comes out of our—mine and my colleague Chris Cousins's—sincere desire to help our clients. How our planning approach transforms people, urges them to think, and changes some of the most important dynamics of their lives is extremely rewarding to me. One client said, "This process frustrates me. I love it and I hate it. I've been goal oriented all of my life and things were achieved. This process pushes me in a direction that I can't necessarily pinpoint and it frustrates me, but it's a good frustration."

Most of all, we make people *think* about big ideas, a process that's vital, but isn't emphasized enough in today's world. We encourage people to *plan*, another practice that's good for our world. These two actions—thinking and planning—lead people to dream up many charitable ideas that are then created and implemented by individuals and families. By thoughtfully planning your life and legacy, you may be able to have a greater impact on the world than you've ever imagined.

I view my involvement in The Family Legacy Center as doing something good for the world. That's good for my industry, good for people, and good for families.

Do you have to create a business to have a positive impact on the world? Of course not. Though many businesses can operate for profit while bringing good into the world.

A person's time can be a charitable endeavor. Think of the moms you know who volunteer in their child's classroom for five hours each week. I was the parent-teacher organization president for a few years and some of those moms are just incredible!

One of our children is on a local competitive jump rope team. My husband and I are constantly noticing how amazing the coaches of the Jumpin' All-Stars (jumpinallstars.org) are. They put in more time with these kids on a weekly basis than I would venture to say many parents spend with their own children. Seriously unreal! Their passion is their team, their creation, their kids. I'll forever connect jump roping with The Jumpin' All-Stars. It's passion and dedication like these coaches possess that begin legacies whether we, or they, realize it or not.

Perhaps your donation is your knowledge. My friend Erica, who was mentioned earlier in connection with her successful business Gal Friday, donates her skills in web design to local teens. It's her way of doing what she can, sharing some of her knowledge and giving back.

Perhaps you've established a charitable foundation. Think of those families or individuals that have established enormous and/or powerful family foundations with a laser focus on a product, passion or idea. These can be enormous undertakings that draw on not just your dollars, but also your heart and soul. Think as big as you'd like.

Point being—charitable involvement can be rather small or incredibly large. With charitable endeavors, I've noticed that what begins small typically grows over a lifetime. Charitable giving also often correlates with rising family wealth. Wealth, i.e., resources, allows you the ability to give more and give more often. For example, wealth can provide the ability to create foundations that can be sustained over many years.

So, just because you have the resources, does that make you charitably inclined? Only you know the answer to that. We all probably know someone with what we would consider vast wealth or resources who doesn't appear inclined to help others. Remember that sometimes charitable giving doesn't have a public face. Many who give prefer to do so anonymously. Many who give might be doing so with intra-family gifts that we never hear about. The bottom line is that the owners of the wealth have the choices to do or not do with it what they deem fit.

Whether you have time, money, or both to share with others, charitable endeavors always come down to personal choice. Consider the ways you can enrich the world around you.

CHALLENGE QUESTION:

Is there something you've wanted to do to "give back" to the world? Now is the time to start. Take baby steps if necessary! The important thing is to start; take that first step.

Epilogue

My hopes.

I hope my message makes you think a little bit.
I hope it makes you plan a little bit.

I hope your children learn from you.
I hope that *you* learn from you.

I hope you enjoy life and get all you can from it. It goes quickly.

I hope you spend the time to give your children tips.
I hope your children listen.

I hope you got a little kick in the pants from reading—the same kind of reminders I get from my husband and my colleague Chris. Tough-love reminders are good for all of us, even if our reflex is to resist.

I hope to hear from you: joanne@financialarch.com.

www.thefamilylegacycenter.com

Reader's Notes

Made in the USA
San Bernardino, CA
25 August 2014